socks appeal

16 fun & funky friends sewn from socks

brenna maloney

stashBOOKS

an imprint of C&T Publishing

Text copyright © 2010 by Brenna Maloney

Artwork copyright © 2010 by C&T Publishing, Inc.

Photography copyright © 2010 by Chuck Kennedy

Publisher: Amy Marson

Creative Director: Gailen Runge

Acquisitions Editor: Susanne Woods

Editor: Cynthia Bix

Technical Editor: Teresa Stroin

Copyeditor/Proofreader: Wordfirm Inc.

Cover/Book Designer: Kristen Yenche

Production Coordinator: Kirstie L. Pettersen

Production Editor: Julia Cianci

Illustrator: Brenna Maloney

Photography by Chuck Kennedy

Published by Stash an imprint of C&T Publishing, Inc., P.O. Box 1456, Lafayette, CA 94549

Library of Congress Cataloging-in-Publication Data

Maloney, Brenna.

  Socks appeal : 16 fun & funky friends sewn from socks / Brenna Maloney.

     p. cm.

  ISBN 978-1-60705-194-7 (soft cover)

  1. Soft toy making. 2. Socks. I. Title.

  TT174.3.M363 2010

  745.592'4--dc22

                              2009048599

Printed in China

10 9 8 7 6 5 4 3 2 1

dedication

This book is dedicated to Meems.

acknowledgments

I'd like to thank the entire team at C&T Publishing. A finer group of creative minds clearly could not exist. A special thanks to my sister, Lisa, who is a shining example of all things fair and decent in the world. Thank you to my parents, two people I rely on and cherish, who are often the source of my most creative thoughts. Loving thanks to my husband, who patiently shot the beautiful photographs for this book and who did not have me committed after getting a look at how many socks we actually have in our basement. And finally I give thanks to my sons, who bluntly told me when an "arm" really looked like a flipper. The two of you drive me and energize me and are, truly, the reason for everything.

contents

ODE TO SOCKS 7

Where to Go for Socks 8

Skills and Instructions 12

Things You Might Need (Besides Socks) 14

EASY-PEASY:
Projects for Beginners & Children. . . 17

Snake 18

Caterpillar. 26

Fish. 32

Turtle 38

Leftover Bits: Jellyfish 42

Starfish 44

LOOK MA, NO HANDS!
Projects for Intermediates

Projects for Intermediates 48

Rabbit. 50

Penguin 64

Owl. 68

Baby Cat. 74

Hamster 78

Lion. 84

Mouse 92

PASS THE EXCEDRIN:
More Challenging Projects

More Challenging Projects 97

Dinosaur. 98

Squirrel. 104

Octopus 112

Mermaid. 120

FINAL THOUGHTS 126

ABOUT THE AUTHOR 127

ode to socks

I don't actually *have* a foot fetish. When a person owns as many socks as I now seem to, you might begin to wonder. But no, I'm not really into feet. And I'm certainly not into socks as footwear. In fact, I would discourage you from wearing socks at all.* Why would you waste a perfectly good pair of socks on your *feet* when you could turn that pair into something much more interesting?

My earnest desire, if you must know, is to dissuade you and any other readers from The Wearing of The Socks. You need to understand that socks have a higher purpose than merely warming your tootsies.

Now, I know you *must* realize this, deep down; otherwise you'd never be in possession of this book. And you must be feeling a little guilty, right? Because you've been wearing them, haven't you? You've been wearing the socks, knowing that they were meant for better things. It's okay. I'm not going to judge you. In fact, I'm here to help.

I'll be honest with you: I have no special powers whatsoever. I am just a normal person, like you or like Jennifer Aniston, minus the incredible wealth and ample boobage, of course. But you and I must be a little bit alike, aren't we? When you're putting on your socks in the morning, do you pause? When buying socks, do you gravitate toward brightly colored ones, even though they don't match anything in your wardrobe? Do you occasionally pass by your sock drawer with a pair of scissors? It's okay to admit it; you're among friends.

Here's the good news: You don't have to be a master sewer to make a one-of-a-kind creation from a sock. All you need are a few basic supplies—socks being the most vital—and about 30 minutes. Now, don't blame me if you find yourself spending much more time than that. It's not as addictive as coffee, but once you master the basics, you may be hooked and no sock will be safe!

This book can tell you what to do with holey socks or orphaned socks or even that brand-new pair of glittery toe socks your sister just gave you. If it can go on your feet, you can learn to transform it into a creative stuffed toy.

Ready to get started?

Unless you live in Duluth, Minnesota. Then you are allowed to wear at least two pairs, year round.

where to go for socks

Well, what are those on your feet?

You don't really need them do you? As socks, I mean. Take them off. Let's size them up. We can probably make something with those. Stop being such a baby. Take them off, now; we're going to need them.

But, that's only one pair, and we will need more than that, so where can we go? Well…you could try raiding someone's sock drawer, I suppose. Not that I am condoning thievery or anything. It's really a matter of perspective. You need to think of it as "liberating" the socks of others. Yes, that's right. You are freeing these socks for that higher calling we spoke of earlier.

Loved ones make good targets— spouses, roommates, friends— although you didn't hear that from me. In my case, I went straight to my husband's sock drawer.

His sock drawer is in a constant state of disarray. I sincerely doubted he would even notice a missing sock. On the off-chance that he did, I was ready with an alibi: I would blame the washer. It's called "plausible deniability." I imagined it like this:

Husband: "Honey, have you seen my gray sock?"

Me: "You're holding it, dear."

Husband, initially perplexed: "Oh, no. I mean the match to this one."

Me: "Well, heavens no. The washer probably ate it. You know what a beast that thing is."

Husband: "Really?"

Me: "Yes, yes. You should go down there right now and try to fix that thing."

Husband: "Oh. Okay."

In truth, he never noticed at all. However, the reality was that his sock drawer was not terribly interesting, and I quickly became aware of the drawbacks to my plan. First: The color selection was dismal. His collection included black, gray, another kind of gray, and gray that used to be white. Nasty. Second: The state of the socks found in his drawer was appalling. Can you spell H-O-L-E-S?

I had to wonder how he could even put them on, day after day, without saying something. Maybe you will have better luck with your loved ones, but as for me, his sock drawer was *not* a good option.

You may have to do what I did: buy them. I'm a bit of a savage and have no pride whatsoever. I will shop for socks anywhere: garage sales, gas stations, department stores, convenience stores. Probably my most reliable source is Target. Target is reasonably priced, has a lot of sales, and often sells socks in bulk. What's not to love? Look for socks in all sections of the store: Go to the men's, women's, kids, toddler, and baby aisles. Because all of these categories of people are known to wear socks.

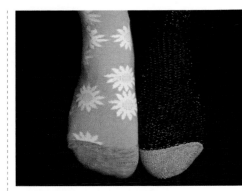

Some socks are better than others. Well, maybe not when you are starting out, but after you've made a bazillion rabbits, as some of us here might actually have done, you will start to get a little snobby about your materials.

I will save you a few headaches here and tell you to steer clear of socks made mostly of nylon. Far too stretchy and slick when you are sewing the little buggers. Socks that are 100 percent cotton are a little clunky to work with. Look for a poly/cotton blend with a hint of spandex or Lycra. This will get you started. Once you get your sea legs, you'll want to experiment with weirder things—knobby wool socks, socks made from bamboo, microfiber socks—and I wholeheartedly encourage you to do so.

Let's take a little peek at a few socks, just to get you up to speed.

Baby sock

Sure, you'll go blind trying to make something cute out of this. But, man, will it be cute when you succeed.

Two-toed sock

Okay, I really have no earthly idea what to do with this one. But don't you think it's cool?

Toe sock

Should *never* be worn on feet; best use is as a sock creature.

Anklet
I hold these in contempt; I really do. More on this later.

Crew sock
This is your bread and butter, right here. You can do anything with a crew sock.

Knee-high
The longer the sock, the more things you can make from it!

note

Never, ever, ever throw away any leftover sock bits. Store them in a bag or a box or keep them under your mattress. You can always use them as paws or ears or tails on other sock creatures. For example, see Jellyfish, on page 42. Or Mouse, page 92.

skills and instructions

Having me as a guide could be disastrous for you. I never seem to use the proper words for things. A typical exchange with my husband might go like this:

Me: "I can't find the thing to zap the whatsit with so I can find my way to the place."

Him: "Oh, you can't find the charger for the GPS so you can navigate to Jo-Ann Fabrics?"

Me: "That's what I said!"

Being a regular person such as yourself, I do not have the craft vocabulary of, say, a Martha Stewart. I personally find some sewing and craft books very intimidating, to the point of MEGO*: *Align dart A with point B at section C with pattern D, being careful not to...* "zzzzzzzzzzzzzz...oh, I'm sorry! Were you saying something?" Sigh. So, yes, the instructions *are* written in *Brennaspeak*, but I have honestly tried to write them as clearly as possible.

MEGO: my eyes glaze over

A WORD ABOUT THE SEWING

I used a sewing machine—my trusty Kenmore—to sew the bodies of most of these beasties. I use the most basic straight stitch the machine has, nothing fancy. No need to use zigzag or get artsy with it.

Now, that's not to say that the bodies can't be hand-sewn. If you want to, you can use a basic running stitch to sew the pieces together. You don't even need to overcast the edges unless you have a particularly ravelly type of sock. (Is that a word? I'm not sure it is, but you get the idea.)

Even though I stitched the bodies together on the machine, I did the detail work by hand—stitching the bodies closed after stuffing using a slip stitch or a ladder stitch (see page 13), attaching the arms, then affixing the eyes.

Once the bodies and appendages were finished, I used simple embroidery stitches to create the faces. And I do mean simple. Now, if you were thinking that this book would dazzle you with advanced sewing skills, I must disappoint. My skills are remedial at best. I rely only on a handful of stitches that my mother taught me when I was nine or so. At right are a few diagrams. I drew them myself, so, sorry for any artistic lameness, but hopefully they will help you a little.

STITCH GALLERY

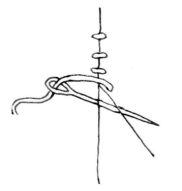

Slip stitch

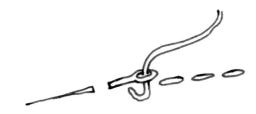

Running stitch

Ladder stitch

Satin stitch

Backstitch

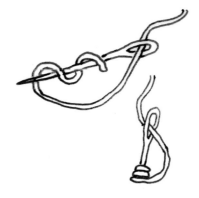

French knot

things you might need (besides socks)

There are a few embellishments and tools you might like to have on hand while working with socks, beyond the basics of needle, thread, scissors, rotary cutter and mat, and stuffing. I don't use a particular brand of polyfil, just whatever I can find at craft or fabric stores. I use pencils or chopsticks to push the stuffing into the hard-to-reach places. Or, you can try using Alex Anderson's 4-in-1 Essential Sewing Tool (available from C&T Publishing) for stuffing.

Buttons: great eyes for mid- to large-scale creatures

Beads: best for eyes on small creatures; can also be used as embellishments on fish and mermaids

Ribbon: keen for manes, fish spines

DMC floss (2 to 3 strands): essential for embroidering faces

Yarn: good for manes, tails, other embellishments

Invisible marker: helpful in marking patterns

RULES TO SEW BY

Now before I set you loose, I'd better give you a few rules to follow. Remember, as a regular ole person who gets easily distracted by, well, just about anything, I might forget to tell you something important right in the middle of a project. So here are a few things to remember as you work:

- Turn socks inside out when you cut and stitch body parts together.

- Always leave a gap of ½" to 1" when you stitch the body, so you can turn it right side out before stuffing.

- Stuff fully but don't pack too tight.

- Use a slip stitch to close up the gap after stuffing.

- To hand stitch arms and other appendages to the beasties' bodies, fold under the raw edge and use a slip stitch.

- Try to maintain a ¼" seam allowance on most of these projects. For some of the smaller projects, like Owl, you might need to dip below this.

- Don't run with scissors, no matter how excited you are about your socks.

CAUTION

Finally, let's talk about screwups. Now, there's going to be *suckitude*, there just is. And I don't want you to get down about it. Sometimes, despite our best efforts, a pattern just comes out looking funky. Maybe the sock was too stretchy or you were distracted by multitasking (sewing while washing the dog while helping with fifth-grade long-division homework while dressing for work, etc.). This happens. You don't know how many weird things I have accidentally created in this manner. Sometimes it is salvageable, sometimes not. If something turns out positively hideous, just put it away for a while. If it doesn't look better to you in a few hours or a few days or after a bout of heavy drinking, then you may need to give it a toss. Or, as my sister would say: File it in the circular file (trash can). It happens to the best of us. Shake it off. Move on.

easy-peasy: projects for beginners & children

You're going to have fun. There's just no way around it. The only danger with these simple patterns is that you won't be able to stop yourself. I dare you to make only one fish. You won't be able to do it. You'll make a green one, and then you'll want to make a blue striped one, and then you'll want to try one with crazy fins, and then, well, trust me, it's really hard to stop. Snake, Caterpillar, Fish, Starfish, and Turtle are all wonderful patterns for beginners and children learning to sew. And to help you with all your leftover sock bits, I've added a super-easy pattern for Jellyfish.

Designed and made by Brenna Maloney

snake

Finished size: about 13″
(if you use a knee-high sock)

The knee-high sock, you will find, is good for many things. Not for wearing, of course. Good grief, no. Who wants to wear a sock that high? Are your calves really going to get cold? What sort of pants are you wearing? *That* may be the problem right there. No, I suggest you put those knee-highs of yours to a much better use: Turn them into snakes!

instructions

For information about hand stitching, see page 13.

The snake is a fun pattern that is a good one to try with kids. Any sock will do, but let's choose a nice, long knee-high. We'll pick a striped one.

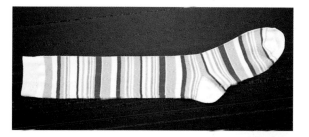

As this is the very first pattern in this book, I wanted to ensure success. So I recruited the help of a slightly unwilling four-year-old, figuring that if he and I could do it, it should be no problem for you at all.

1. My able assistant was quick to tell me that a snake is long and straight, so remove any sock parts that give you trouble in this regard. Go ahead and cut off the foot of the sock, and if the end of the cuff is, as we judged ours to be, "too lumpy," you may want to lop that off as well.

2. Unless you want a very fat snake, pare him down a little on the sides, and while you are at it, shape his head and tail. You do this by rounding his head and trimming his tail into a point. Now he should look good and snakelike.

3. A snake needs a tongue to hiss with, so hunt up an inch or two of narrow ribbon for this. We used a ⅛" ribbon, but you could also use ¼" ribbon.

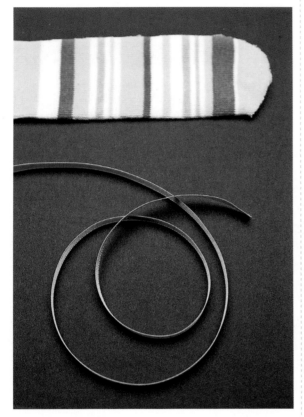

4. Cut a length of ribbon about 2" long. Turning your snake inside out, place the ribbon at the center of his head between the top and bottom layers, with most of the ribbon facing inward. Pin the ribbon in place.

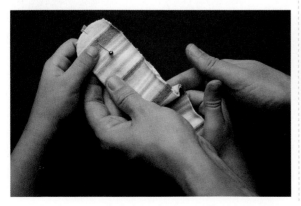

5. Sew the top and bottom pieces together, but as you do so, leave a small gap—maybe 1" long—so that you can turn him right side out. I've found that if you leave this opening about midway down the snake, he will be easier to stuff.

6. Turn the snake right side out and begin stuffing. You can start on either end; it doesn't matter. Stuff him evenly on each end until you get to the opening.

7. Stitch the opening together using a matching thread and a slip stitch.

8. Mr. Snake would love a pair of eyes. We used size 6 glass seed beads, but you can use small buttons, felt circles, or even glue-on google eyes.

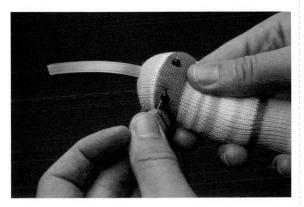

9. Your last step is to put the fork into Snake's forked tongue by snipping a V into the end of the ribbon.

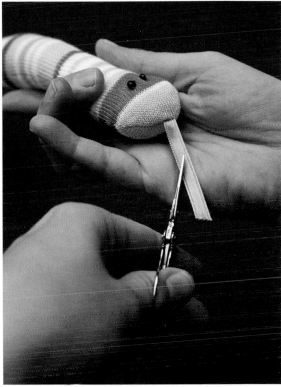

And there you have it!

You can do a lot to alter Snake's appearance.

For a twist, let's add a twist! Here's how:

Form a loop at the end of a pipe cleaner and insert it into your snake's body, with the loop at his head end, before you stuff him. After you stuff him and stitch up the opening, you can twist him into shape.

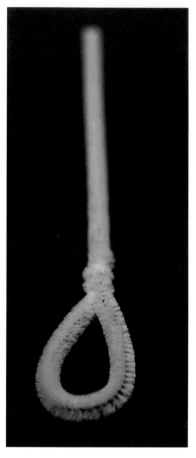

Coiled like a cobra!

All in knots

Or Snake met with an unfortunate accident
and has become roadkill.

Or maybe Snake is besieged by her hungry babies!

Maybe Snake has had a big lunch.

Designed and made by Brenna Maloney

caterpillar

Finished size: about 13″ long

For Caterpillar, we're just going to adjust the snake pattern slightly (page 18). Take a look.

instructions

For information about hand stitching, see page 13.

1. Start out with a knee-high. A striped one, if you have it. Cut off the foot and top cuff.

2. Shape the head and tail, just as we did for Snake. Separate the 2 pieces and lay 1 flat.

3. Caterpillar will need legs that we will place in every other stripe. Choose a slightly stiff, ¼"-wide ribbon. Cut the ribbon into 5" segments. In our case, we have 3 blue stripes on our caterpillar, so I cut 3 lengths of ribbon.

4. The ribbons are going to form her feet. I pinned each end of ribbon to the middle of each blue stripe on both sides of the flat bottom piece. Do this for each darker colored (blue, in our case) stripe.

5. This next step is a little indelicate, so my apologies go to the caterpillar. Fold down the ribbon loop to keep it out of the way of sewing, and cover it with the top piece of the caterpillar. Pin all the way around to hold everything in place.

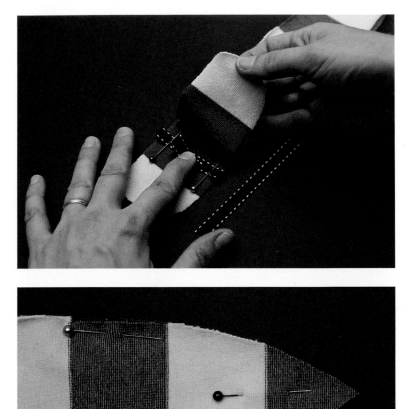

6. Just as with Snake, stitch the top and bottom pieces together (with the ribbon mashed inside), making sure to leave a small opening on her side so you can turn her right side out.

7. When you turn Caterpillar right side out, you are going to get a strange-looking thing, which may make you question my ability to write instructions.

Have no fear! Take your scissors and snip each ribbon loop in half.

Ahhh…does that look any better now? There is a method to my madness! Instant legs!

8. Stuff Caterpillar as you did Snake (page 20), stuffing both ends until you come to the middle. Slipstitch the opening closed.

9. Now we need to accentuate her segments, which is really a lofty way of telling you to get out a needle and thread for a little running stitch. Here I used a matching blue thread and a standard needle to run around each of her stripes.

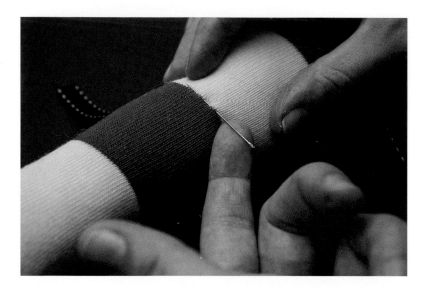

Pull the thread in tight to gather up the sock and knot it securely. Think of it as cinching her into a corset!

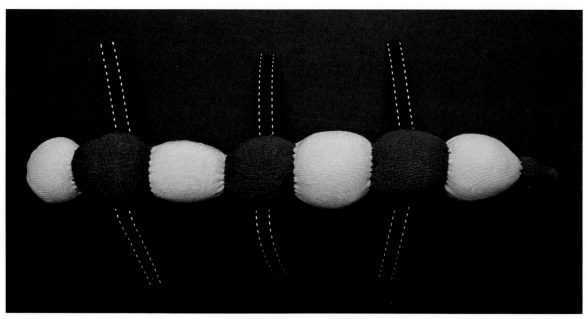

10. She'd like some eyes and a mouth. I used seed beads for her eyes. Try 2 to 3 strands of embroidery floss to backstitch a line for her mouth. (See page 13 for embroidery stitches.)

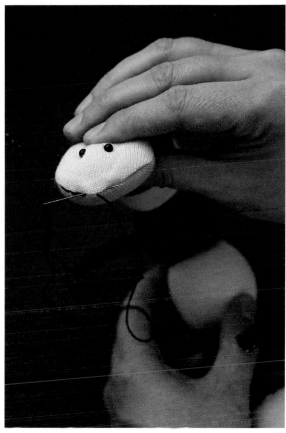

11. One last step: She'd like a pedicure! Using tiny scissors, cut the tips of her ribbon toes into a V, and voila!

Designed and made by Brenna Maloney

fish

Finished size: about 4½″ to 6½″

Let's talk about anklets. What is the point? Only your shoe can see them. Why, you put those things on and you might even forget you are wearing socks. "Honey, do you have socks on today?" "Well, I don't know, dear. Let me look inside my shoe and check." No, I really don't have much use for The Wearing of The Anklets. But darn it all if Target isn't always selling them—and selling them at ridiculous prices: 5 for $5. Well, that's 50 cents a foot, now isn't it? But then you are stuck with the silly things…stuck until…until you decide to repurpose them…as fish!

The fish is another really good pattern to try with kids. Lucky for me, I had the able assistance of a very accomplished six-year-old. I want to prove to you how flexible the fish really is. You can do anything to him and he doesn't mind a bit. Pick a sock, any sock—it can be an anklet, but it can also be a crew sock or a knee high—it doesn't matter. I've given you a few standard fish patterns to try (see page 37), but you probably won't need them, you creative devil, you. Just eyeball it. What does a fish look like? As long as it has a head and a tail fin, you're probably in the ball park.

instructions

For information about hand stitching, see page 13.

1. Feeling unsure? Okay. Let's start with one of the patterns (see page 37). And, for the sake of argument, let's say we'll use the anklet, but only because I know you have so many of them.

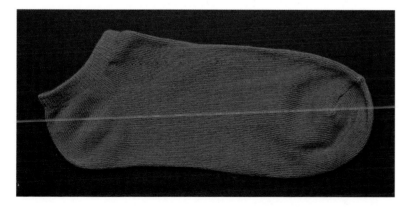

$2.$ Turn your anklet inside out and trace around the pattern with a fabric marker.

$3.$ Cut out your fish.

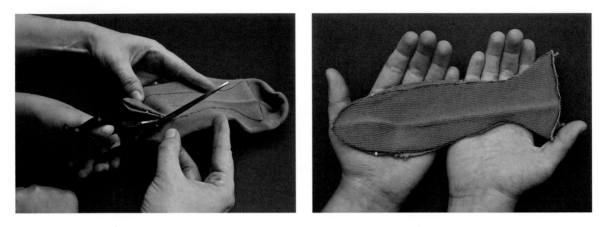

$4.$ Sew Mr. Fish together, making sure to leave a little opening—½" wide or so—under his tummy so that you can turn him.

$5.$ Turn him right side out and begin stuffing. It doesn't matter which end you start from, head or tail, but stuff both ends until you meet in the middle.

$6.$ Using matching thread, slipstitch the opening closed. This fella needs some eyeballs—seed beads, buttons, what have you. And now, you are done. How easy was *that*!

How many fish in the sea?

A gazillion, at least. Once you make the basic pattern, then you can begin to branch out a little and have fun.

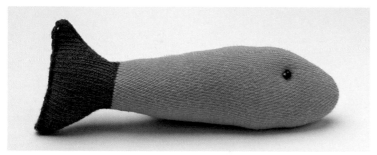

Basic fish

Add spikes!

Add fins!

Add *bling!*

Change his shape!

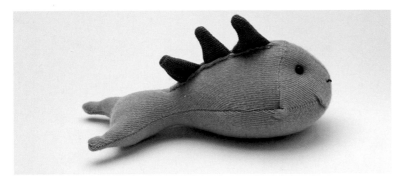

Alter his tail and give him a dorsal fin.

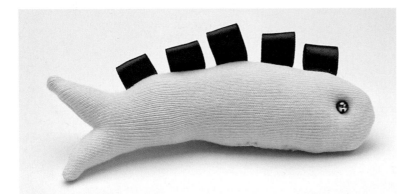

Give him a ribbon fin.

Make something really weird that only vaguely resembles a fish that will cause your loved ones to look at you and do that raised-eyebrow thing!

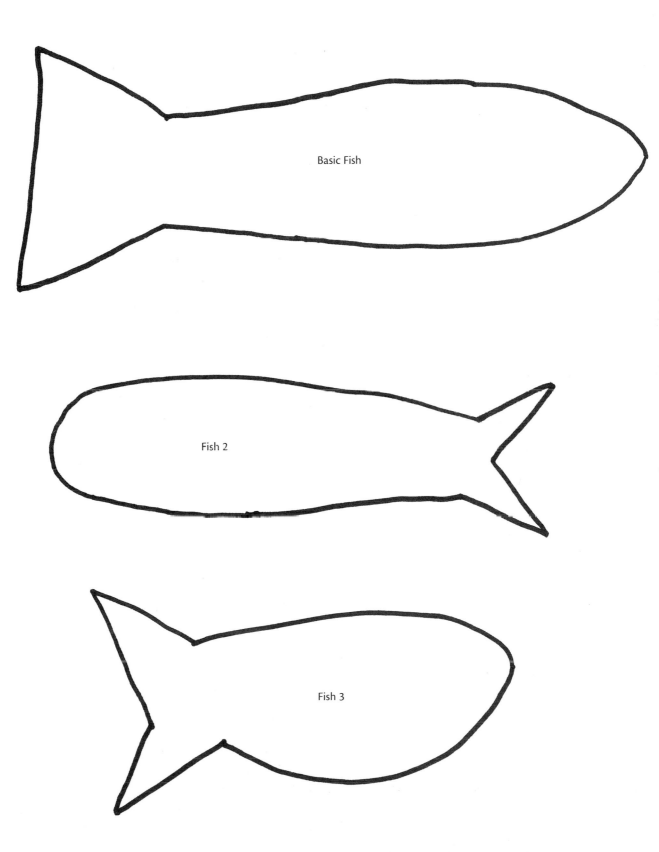

Basic Fish

Fish 2

Fish 3

Designed and made by Brenna Maloney

turtle

Finished size: about 6″ long

Now you're ready to branch out. For Turtle, you are going to need two socks that do not match.

instructions

For information about hand stitching, see page 13.

1. We'll stay away from anklets and go with the ole reliable crew sock.

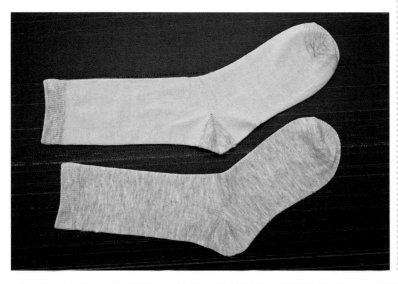

2. Cut an oval from the toe/ instep segment of the first sock. This will form his body and can be almost the full width of the sock.

3. Turn the sock inside out. The next sock will be used for Turtle's head, feet, and tail. Cut the foot segment off this other sock. Here you are going to sew freehand—just by eyeballing it—2 front feet, 2 back feet, a pointed tail, and a head.

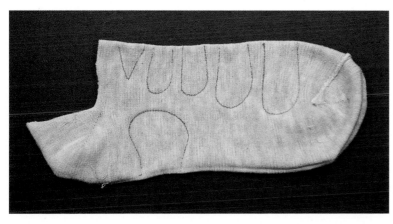

note

Now, stay calm. It's going to be all right. You *can* do this. It doesn't have to be perfect; in fact, your turtle will be so much cuter if things are a little out of whack. I deliberately made one foot much bigger than the others just to make you more comfortable (uh huh, *sure* I did). I used a fabulous orange-colored thread here—not because I am color-blind, but only so that you can see the stitches better. This way, you won't think I've done some fancy stitch magic that leaves you in the dark about how to make Turtle's appendages. (Full disclosure: I don't actually know any fancy stitch magic, so the odds of you being in the dark on my account are slim to none. Just saying.) You'll probably want to use a matching thread because *you* know what you are doing.

4. Once sewn, you can cut these pieces free, cut open the folded edge on each piece, and turn them.

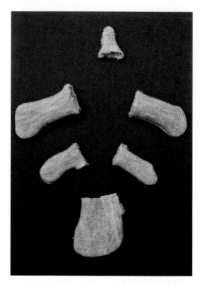

5. This next part is a little dicey, but I think you'll be fine. You're going to make a little turtle sandwich. Fold back the top layer of Turtle's body and insert his head facing inward.

6. Pin the top layer of the body on top to hold everything in place. You are going to repeat this move for his feet and his tail.

7. Once you have everything sandwiched in, you can sew all the layers together, remembering, of course, to leave a small opening in his side so you can turn him.

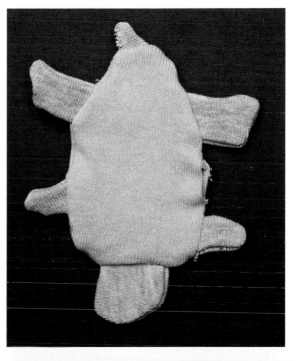

8. Gently stuff Turtle, slipstitch him closed, and give him a pair of bead eyes.

LEFTOVER BITS: JELLYFISH

Designed and made by Brenna Maloney

Finished size: about 13″ long

As I said earlier, if you do enough of these beasties, you'll soon find yourself with a stack of sock parts. I found that I had amassed an odd collection of heels that I didn't know what to do with. I discovered that they can make nice jellyfish.

It's simple!

INSTRUCTIONS

For information about hand stitching, see page 13.

1. Take your odd sock part and cut away everything but the heel.

2. Using a running stitch in a matching thread, turn the raw edges under and stitch around the edges of the heel.

3. Pull gently on the thread to cinch the circle a little (leave the needle and thread in), and stuff. You won't need much stuffing.

4. Now it becomes a small ball. Cinch the ball closed with a strong knot at the end of your thread.

5. Look through your yarn and ribbon collection and find some scraps to use for the tentacles. The stranger, the better. You want a lot of different textures, so try an assortment of craft yarns, ribbon, raffia, cording—whatever you can think of. They can be different lengths, with the longest no more than 12" long.

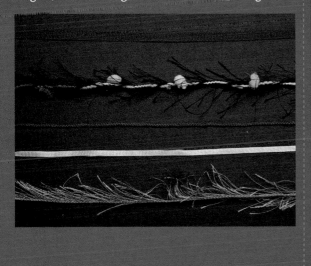

6. Gather the strands together and knot them so you will have long and short tentacles.

7. Insert the knot of strands into the end of the body. You can stitch it in place to hold it or, if you're good with a glue gun, seal it that way.

Designed and made by Brenna Maloney

starfish

Finished size: about 5½" across

In my continued quest to repurpose every last anklet on the planet, let's try our next project, the starfish. The pattern, if you want to use it, is on page 47.

instructions

For information about hand stitching, see page 13.

1. You'll need both socks for this project.

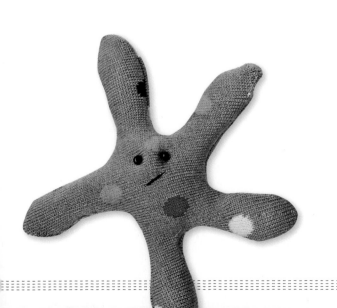

2. Slice each anklet down the bottom.

3. Spread each one out like a butterfly.

4. Using the pattern on page 47 (or, if you are feeling brave, forget the pattern and just eyeball it!), trace the starfish shape with a fabric marker onto the wrong side of one of the socks.

5. Put the socks right sides together and pin so they don't slip. Cut out the starfish.

6. Sew the top and bottom pieces right sides together, being careful to leave a small opening (about ½″) so you can turn her.

7. If you have any difficulties turning the starfish because her limbs are so small, try using an unsharpened pencil or a chopstick to help you push the fabric.

8. When you are ready to stuff her, you can use the same technique with the pencil, this time helping you to gently pack the stuffing in those hard-to-reach places. Don't overstuff her; keep her a little on the flat side.

9. Close the opening with a slip stitch. Add some beads for eyes. Use a backstitch with 2 or 3 strands of embroidery floss for a mouth. (See page 13 for embroidery stitches.)

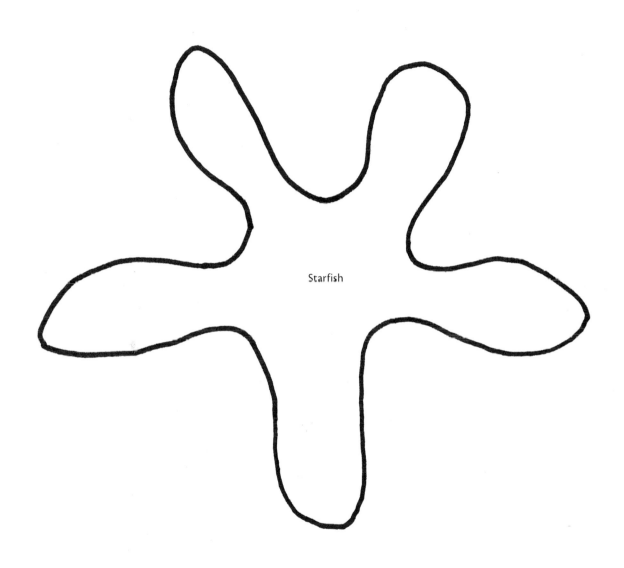

Starfish

look ma, no hands!
projects for intermediates

Take off those training wheels, my friend. If you've managed a little success with any of the patterns from the first section of this book, you're probably ready to try your hand at Rabbit, Penguin, Owl, Baby Cat, Mouse, Hamster, or Lion. These patterns are a little more challenging, but nothing you can't handle. Well, Owl might make you swear like a sailor, but really, that's it. That, and Lion's mane. Seriously. These patterns are fun, and they will give you a chance to add special touches to make them uniquely yours.

Designed and made by Brenna Maloney

rabbit

Finished size: about 9″ tall (excluding the ears)

I have a real affection for the rabbit, I have to tell you. My parents, you see, are very gifted souls who, through their own creative endeavors, taught their children to look at ordinary things in extraordinary ways. As a child, my favorite toys were ones that my parents made for me: a wooden marionette, a doll house, stuffed animals of every sort—monkeys, mice, bears, and, as it happened, a rabbit made from a pink sock. I named her Barbara, and I loved her fiercely. I loved her so hard, in fact, her face nearly came off. Good grief, just look at the poor thing now.

She's as flat as a pancake, all fuzzed up, with half a face. And I love her still. So, you really must learn to make one. You really must. It's good for the soul. I promise.

instructions

For information about hand stitching, see page 13.

1. You'll need a pair of socks for the rabbit. Crew socks will do nicely, of any color or pattern. We'll go with a nice blue, and though it's blue, we'll decide here and now that she is to be a girl rabbit. It is sometimes fun to find a sock that has a contrasting heel, as we have here.

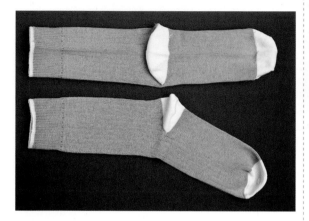

2. Lay the first sock out flat with the heel facing up. Cut vertically down the middle of the sock from the toe to just above the start of the heel. You are creating her ears.

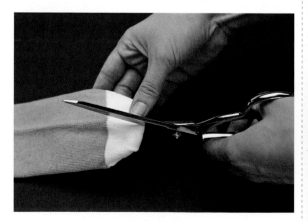

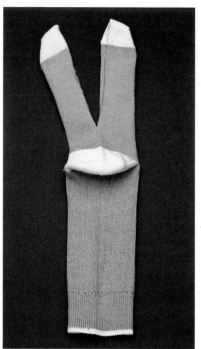

3. On the **second** sock, snip the toe section off and cut it in half. These pieces will form her arms.

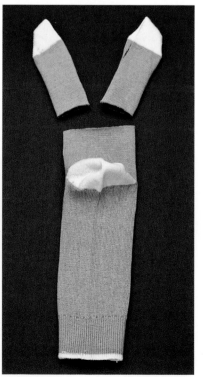

4. For Rabbit's tail, take what is left of the second sock and fold the heel in half. Cut a curved piece to form a circle. You can set this aside for now.

5. Turn Rabbit's body inside out. With right sides together, stitch along her ears from one toe tip to the other. Then stitch each arm with right sides together. Turn her right side out again; she's ready to be stuffed. Turn Rabbit's body (the first sock) inside out. With right sides together, stitch along her ears from one toe tip to the other. Then stitch each arm with right sides together. Turn her body and arms right side out again; she's ready to be stuffed. Set the arms aside for now.

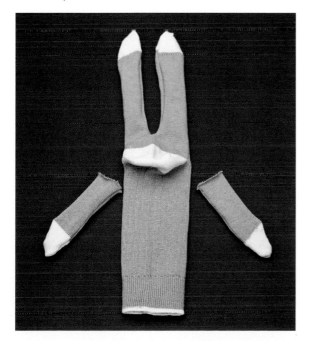

6. Start with her head. You want her to be a little understuffed and squishy, so don't pack the stuffing too tightly. (No need to stuff her ears!)

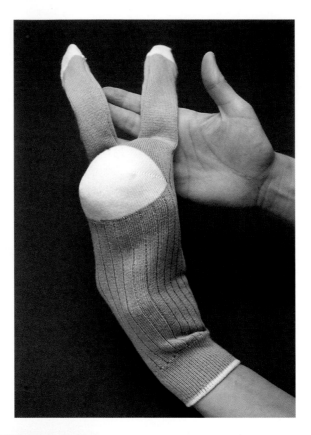

7. Continue stuffing her body until you get to the end of the sock. With needle and matching thread, gather up the end of the sock with a running stitch, and draw the thread together, like closing a drawstring bag.

Depending on how thick your sock is, you might not be able to close the circle completely. (I am notoriously bad at this, in fact.) Knot securely.

8. On to her arms! You don't need to stuff them; simply sew them to the sides of her body. Turn under the raw edges and stitch down with a slip stitch.

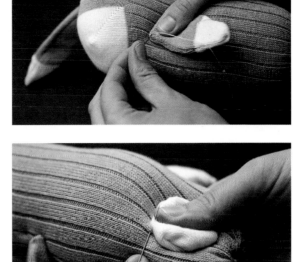

9. Let's add her tail now. Take the circular piece of sock you cut from the heel. Fill it with just a pinch of stuffing. Form a ball by turning in the raw edges, and sew it to her back end using a slip stitch.

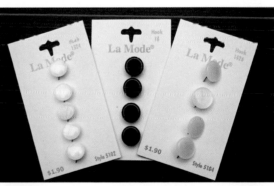

10. She'll need a face, of course. Her eyes can be stitched-on pieces of felt, buttons, or beads, or glue-on google eyes. I like to use buttons with a shank on the back. I mostly use black or white buttons, $7/16"$ or $3/8"$ size.

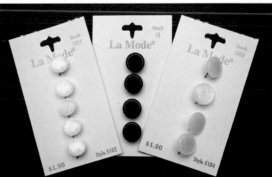

11. For her nose and mouth, choose a shade of pink embroidery floss. Use 2 to 3 strands and satin stitch a triangle nose.

Extend the line from the tip of the nose down about ½" to form the beginning of the mouth. Cross sideways; cross back again. You'll be making an upside-down Y.

Finis!

BABY BUNNY

If you are feeling really adventurous, you can fashion a baby bunny from an infant sock. I took the smallest argyle sock I could find and cut and stitched the ears exactly as you would for the big rabbit. Do a quick running stitch to seal her back end, and she's basically finished! I used French knots for her eyes and a little satin stitch for her nose and mouth. These silly things don't sit up well at all. But they are funny to look at and super simple to make.

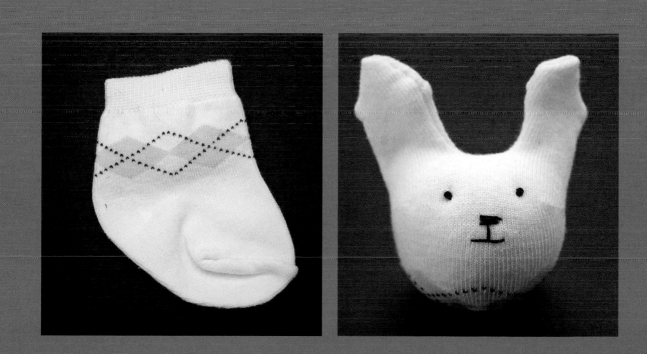

VARIATIONS ON A THEME

I want to impress upon you the flexibility of the Rabbit pattern and encourage you to use your creative genius. I've made a series of white rabbits for you, to help illustrate that how you sew the face will determine what sort of rabbit you really have. Even if you use the same elements as I've used here—black (or red) buttons and embroidery floss—you can get very different looks.

RABBIT #1: With eyes too close together we have a rabbit of suspicious character. Note the thin nose. This rabbit looks shifty to me, perhaps a member of the criminal element? Not to be trusted, at any rate.

RABBIT #2: With eyes slightly askew, we can create an interesting look. Sometimes by sewing one eye higher than the other, the rabbit appears to be turning her face to look up at you. It is a slippery slope though, as I have made rabbits like this before that just end up looking half crazy. So, they either look incredibly endearing or completely mad.

RABBIT #3: With eyes spaced far apart and a wide nose and smile, we have a gentle giant. A dopey, harmless rabbit.

RABBIT #4: Same type of button, but this time a different color. And the nose and mouth match the eye color. I've added whiskers, which may or may not appeal to you.

RABBIT #5: When my mother made Barbara for me, she used button eyes but made the nose from felt and embroidered the rest of the mouth. Felt can really change the rabbit's features. I like the nose as a heart, with the red button eyes. These are the same style of buttons, just a different color again.

Rabbit lineup

Yet more rabbits

Two-tone rabbits

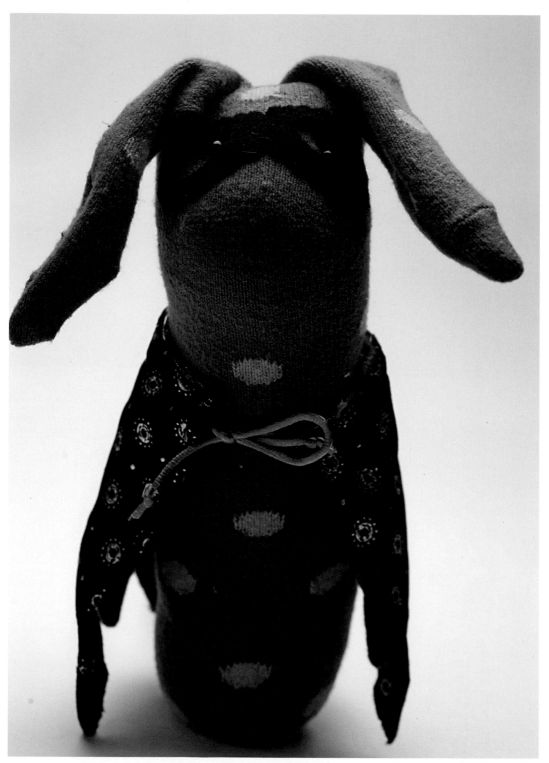

Masked, marauder rabbit

Purple-faced black rabbit

Bling eyed rabbit

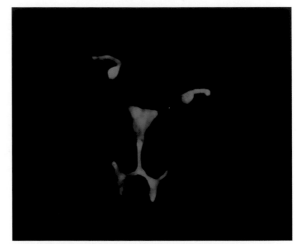

Now you see it, now you don't: rabbit painted with glow-in-the-dark fabric paint!

Mustached rabbit

Designed and made by Brenna Maloney

penguin

Finished size: about 7½″ tall

Penguin is a very sweet pattern and a good one to try if you've made a rabbit (page 50) because the patterns are so similar.

instructions

For information about hand stitching, see page 13.

1. Crew socks work well for this project, and we've a fine stripy pair here. You could also use a knee-high and might then have enough extra sockage that you'd only need to use one sock, not the pair. Either way.

2. The sock-cutting part is slightly tricky. You need to banish Rabbit from your mind for a second, because instead of giving Penguin ears, you are going to create his nose. Cut one sock above the heel to a point, which will become his nose. Think of it this way: His face will be pointing in the opposite direction from that of Rabbit's.

3. From the top of the toe section, cut 2 slanted flippers.

4. From the second sock, cut off the toe, and cut that piece in half to make 2 feet.

5. Turn all these bits and pieces inside out and begin sewing, right sides together. Stitch each set of flippers and feet first, and then stitch along the point on Penguin's head to form his nose.

6. Turn everything right side out and have a look at your penguin's fine nose.

7. Stuff him loosely, and with a running stitch sew up the sock end (his, ahem, butt), just as you did with Rabbit.

8. While you are down there, please attach his feet.

9. And do give him his arms. No need to stuff them; he prefers them flat. He can paddle better that way. Turn under the raw edges and stitch down with a slip stitch.

10. All he lacks are eyes, and I know you'll pick good ones.

Designed and made by Brenna Maloney

owl

Finished size: about 5˝ tall

Now we are going to step gingerly into the world of itty bitty toddler socks. This is not for the faint at heart or those with questionable eyesight. Get out the magnifying glass, my friend, you're going to need it.

Really, any toddler sock will do, but I am partial to striped ones for Owl.

WARNING

Sometimes you will find little speed bump thingies on the bottom of toddler socks. I don't really know what this is all about. Is it supposed to slow your toddler down? Is it supposed to give your toddler Mighty Grippy Powers so he won't fall down as he streaks across the kitchen floor? Here, they read OLD NAVY in big, ridiculous letters. I don't generally let this stress me; I cut and sew as if that isn't even there. But, I do know that this will absolutely agitate some folks, and I can respect that. If you are one of those people—and there's no shame in it—look for toddler socks without the speed bumps.

Now then, if you have any swearing that you need to get out of your system before you start this project, go right ahead. I'll wait. There will be several opportunities later for screaming. But you might feel better if you go ahead now, and then you can go again later, if you need to. I sound like I'm potty training a toddler. Sorry. Okay. Now, what were we talking about? Oh yes, the *owl*.

instructions

For information about hand stitching, see page 13.

1. Okay. You'll only need 1 sock to make the owl. Cut owl's body out of the lower part of this sock, where the cuff is. Just snip right below the heel and give him a rounded head.

2. From the remaining part of the sock, snip the very tip of the toe off and cut that in half. These will form his itty bitty microscopic wings that will make you want to cry for your momma while you try to sew the blasted things on. But, that misery comes later.

3. With the strange piece that is leftover, start from the heel, and cut the sock open.

4. Lay this piece out, and from it, cut the largest oval you can. This will be your owl's butt.

5. Turn Owl's body inside out, with right sides together, and sew the front and back pieces of his rounded little head together. Also sew his wings together and turn them right side out.

6. Go slowly on this next step. Keeping the owl body inside out, pin the oval piece that you cut in Step 4 (the owl's butt) to the open end of his body. Pin the 2 pieces right sides together with raw edges lined up, and stitch around the circle, being careful to leave a small opening so you can turn him.

7. Turn him and stuff his little fat body. Seal the opening with a slip stitch.

8. Hand sew his itty bitty arms to the side of his body. Swearing is optional.

9. The eyes are really going to make your owl, so look carefully for a good match. I chose bright orange buttons for this one. But be on the lookout for buttons or beads that have a ring in the center that can double as a pupil. For a nose, I used a small triangle of felt.

And you are done. Are we still friends?

Designed and made by Brenna Maloney

baby cat

Finished size: about 5½″ tall

Like Owl (page 68), Baby Cat also uses a little kid sock, slightly larger than a toddler sock. It should come without "speed bumps" (see page 69).

instructions

For information about hand stitching, see page 13.

1. You'll be using a pair of socks to produce a cat.

2. There's a bit of fancy footwork here with the cutting, so let me walk you through it. On the first sock, you are going to cut a small V in the toe. This will eventually become his legs. Just above the heel on the same sock, cut across, creating what will be his slightly rounded head. From what is left of the sock and cuff, you can cut 4 small triangles for his ears. As for the second sock, you are going to cut off most of the toe section and cut it in half for his arms, much like you did if you made the rabbit (page 52). Then cut a strip from the heel to form a thin tail.

3. With right sides together, stitch the small triangles together to make 2 pointy ears. Turn his body inside out and insert his ears in the top of his head, points down. Pin and stitch closed the top of his head.

4. With right sides together, sew each arm, and do the same with the tail. Turn everything right side out. Now you have a flat little body with ears and detached arms and a tail. You can leave the entire V open between the legs for stuffing, or you can sew closed the toes and leave a smaller V for stuffing. Whatever you feel comfortable with.

5. Stuff Baby Cat and slipstitch the opening you left to turn him. Do not stuff his arms, but sew them flat to his sides, just as for Rabbit (page 55) and Penguin (page 67).

6. Tack his tail to his caboose.

7. For Baby Cat's face, I used simple lines made with straight stitches and 2 strands of DMC floss. I added whiskers, too. Meow.

Designed and made by Brenna Maloney

hamster

Finished size: about 6½″ tall

Here's our friend, Hamster. You'll need a nice crew sock for him.

instructions

For information about hand stitching, see page 13.

1. I was lucky to find a sock with a banded cuff on it, but yours can be all one color, if that suits you.

2. Cut a large portion of the foot section off, just below the heel. Also, cut off the top of the cuff. The heel will become Hamster's face, and the bottom of the cuff, his body.

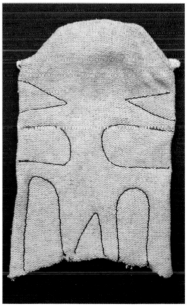

3. Turn the toe section inside out. This will be your canvas to fashion 2 feet, 2 paws, 2 ears, and 1 triangular tail. You are going to sew this free-hand by machine, but I know you are not afraid (especially if you have tackled a similar task by making Turtle, page 38). Just to help out a bit, I used dark thread so that you could clearly see what to do. (Of course, you will want to use thread that matches your sock.) Now remember, you are eyeballing these; they are not going to be perfect, and that is perfectly okay. Cut out the pieces, leaving a ⅛″ margin/seam allowance all around, and turn them right side out.

4. The next bit is a little tricky, so stay with me here. Do you have a rotary cutter? I've found that these can come in handy at times. What we want to do is cut 2 slits, each ½" to ¼" long, in Hamster's chest so that we can slip his paws in and secure them. Place a small piece of cardboard inside Hamster before you cut so you won't slice into his back; you want the cuts just on the front.

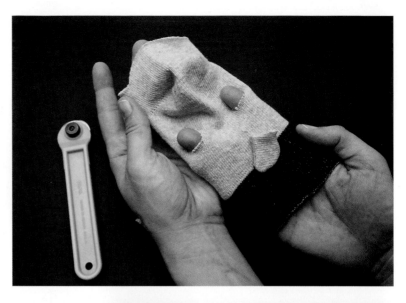

5. Turn Mr. Hamster inside out, insert his paws, and fold his chest in half along the slit, with the paws sandwiched between. Machine stitch these layers together from the wrong side (you can do this by hand, if you prefer). Turn him right side out and admire your work. Don't worry if the sock puckers a bit between his new paws; we can fix that when we stuff him.

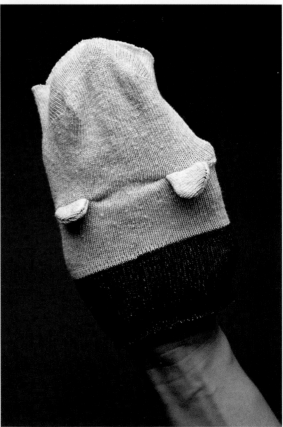

6. Now we are going to attach his ears, so turn him inside out again and pin the ears in place. Pin his ears inside the top of his head, with raw edges matching and pointy ends down, and sew across his head. This should cause you no worries at all because you have done the same if you made Baby Cat (page 75).

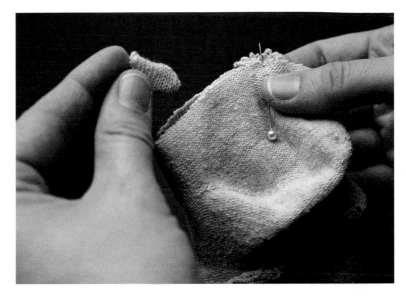

7. Turn Mr. Hamster right side out and go ahead and stuff him. Not too much, or he'll have trouble sitting upright. When he's had enough, gather the ends with a running stitch as for Rabbit (page 54) and Penguin (page 66) and close him up. Don't be worried if you can't sew the opening completely closed. Depending on how thick your sock is, it might be slightly open. Not the end of the world. Now, while you are down there at the business end of Mr. Hamster, you can sew on his little feet and tail.

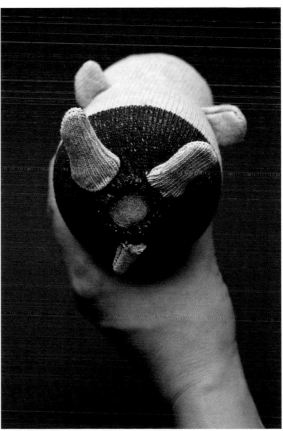

8. He'll want some eyes next. I used black buttons. And for a nose, would you believe I actually glue-gunned a tiny pompon on? I'm a disaster when it comes to glue guns. I always manage to singe one digit or another—still. That's one fine nose, don't you think?

9. A simple backstitch with 3 strands of black DMC will give Hamster a sweet smile and help finish him off.

More hamsters!

Now, you can have a little bit of fun with Hamster's tum, depending on what sort of sock you pick. The banded sock is nice, but take a look at him in argyle...

or polka dot…

or even more fun, a kid's pirate sock!

Designed and made by Brenna Maloney

lion

Finished size: about 17″ tall

Remember during the opening of this book (Caution, page 16 to be exact) I had a little chat with you about failure and potential suckitude? Well, here comes mine: the lion. The lion is a great pattern, but for some reason, I have been foiled by his mane on more than one occasion. I am not worried about this for you. This is my bugaboo, not yours. I think you will succeed effortlessly. He will probably end up being your favorite pattern in the whole book, and I'm okay with that. Sniff, sniff. Just because *I* mess it up doesn't mean that someone else of superior skill can't come along behind me and be brilliant. It's okay. Really.

instructions

For information about hand stitching, see page 13.

1. Depending on your selection, you may only need one sock for Lion. The sock I used is one of those mega knee-high deals—thigh-highs, I think they call them. Let me tell you something: If your thighs are so cold you need socks to warm them, your skirt is too short, sister. You need to go back inside and rethink that outfit and then give your socks to me. Honestly. I thought I had taught you better than that!

2. Don't get into a tizzy over how to cut this big ole sock out. It's really not so bad. Let me walk you through it: First, cut the whole foot off, right below the heel. Split the foot section down the middle to form Lion's arms. Cut the ribbed cuff off, and as I did here, you might want to cut a bit more off so his legs aren't so terribly long. You can make little ears with the extra.

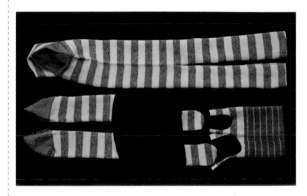

3. Stitch the top and bottom pieces of his ears together and turn them right side out. Turn his body inside out and insert his ears between the layers, points facing down. Sew across the top of his head to close it, and attach the ears.

4. Now sew the rest of his body right sides together, making sure to leave a small opening so you can turn him. Pay particular attention to his feet. I sewed mine straight across. If you want to curve the stitch a little so his big manly feet don't seem so blocky, who am I to stop you?

5. Turn him right side out and begin stuffing. I'll be honest with you: I packed my stuffing pretty tight on this pattern. You don't have to. You might want him a little bit floppy. Mine will forever stand at attention because I got a little carried away with the stuffing and couldn't stop. ("Put the polyfil bag *down*, ma'am! Step awaaaay from the lion.")

6. We've ignored his arms up to now. With right sides together stitch along the open sides of his arms. Turn the arms right side out and—just as we did with Rabbit (page 55)—turn under the raw edges and stitch each arm to the side of Lion's body with a slip stitch.

7. He'll need some eyes now. And a little face. I went wild here with yellow buttons. Hey, for me, that's pretty wild. And the face is a lot like Rabbit's (page 56)— stitched using 2 or 3 strands of black DMC floss.

8. But wait! You aren't finished yet. He's a lion, after all. A fierce jungle cat, on the prowl. Give him some claws! At least on his feet. Get down there with your 2 or 3 strands of black DMC floss and make a few straight stitches.

9. Hold it! You still aren't done. Give him a belly button. Yes, do. Why not? Don't you think he needs one? Just a little French knot in the center of his tum using 2 or 3 strands of black DMC floss. Only takes a minute. And he'll feel so much better. Like so. Yes. Nicely done.

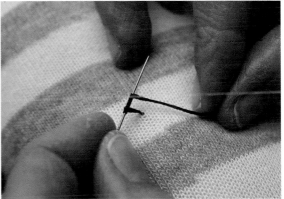

10. Now, the bit I seem to perpetually screw up: the mane. But it's okay. I have faith in you. You are going to breeze through this. Find a couple of yarns you think will work. Put them together in your hand and form a loop. You don't need to cut the yarn yet, just keep it in the skein.

11. Sew this loop onto the edge of Lion's face. Don't cut the yarn—just let it dangle as you sew the first loop. Then make another loop and tack it down. Continue around the face, unwinding yarn off the skein and sewing loops, until you've gone around the whole circle. Work slowly. Keep the swearing to a minimum—you don't want to wake a sleeping lion, believe me.

12. You can use the same yarn for his tail. Just cut 6 or 7 strands, each 5" long. Gather them up and knot them.

13. Tack the knot down to his butt, and Lion is ready to go chase antelope.

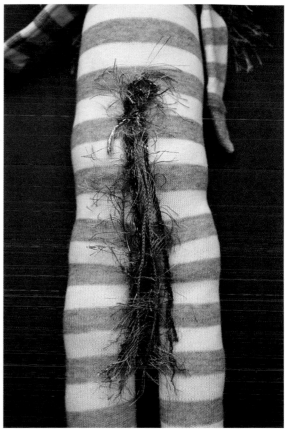

A Word about Manes

There are many things you can use to make a mane. In this project we used yarn. I've had a lot of luck with some of the novelty yarn from Lion Brand Yarn and Yarn Bee.

You can also use feathers, sock strips, novelty trims, ribbons, beads, and sequins.

Feathers

Sock strips

Fancy trim

Designed and made by Brenna Maloney

mouse

Finished size: about 4¼″ long

I managed to find one other use for the odious anklet! Try your hand at this simple, albeit rather flat, mouse.

instructions

For information about hand stitching, see page 13.

1. You'll need 1 especially bright-colored anklet.

2. Cut off the tip of the toe section and set it aside.

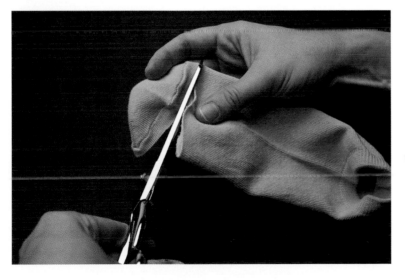

3. With the remaining portion of the sock, use the pattern I have for you below (or eyeball it) to cut out the body of the mouse from the double sock thickness.

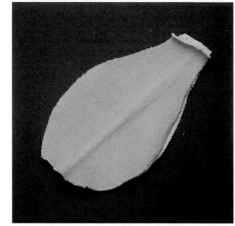

4. Take the cut-off toe portion and turn it inside out. Sew—freehand—2 ears, and turn them right side out again. (If you want to mark the outlines on the sock first, see the examples for Turtle, page 39, or Hamster, page 79.)

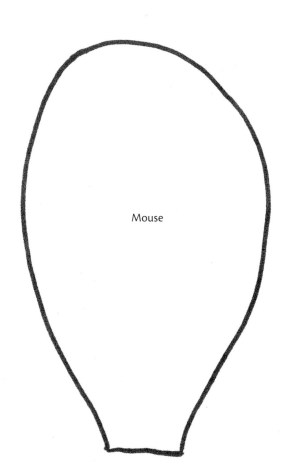

Mouse

5. Grab your handy rotary cutter. Lay the top piece of Mouse's body on a cutting mat and make 2 slits, each ½" wide, in the top of Mouse's head.

6. Fold the corner of his ear inward. Pinch together his ear at the base.

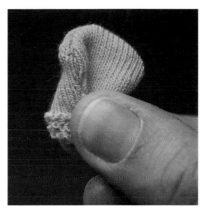

7. Insert the ear in the slit on top of his head and sew it on the wrong side. Then do the other ear.

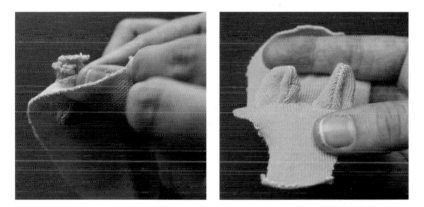

8. Look in your leftover sock pile. Don't pretend that by now you don't have one! Look for a little piece of pink sock that we can use for a nose. Cut out a tiny triangle.

9. Search your stash for a bit of cord or thin ribbon so he'll have a tail. Cut a length and knot the end.

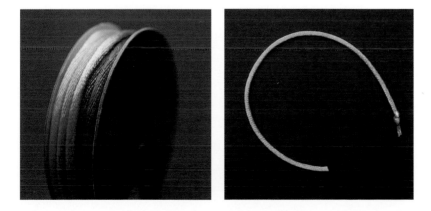

10. Put his top and bottom body pieces right sides together, with the nose piece and tail piece sandwiched in place. Sew around the body: Be sure to leave a small opening so you can turn him.

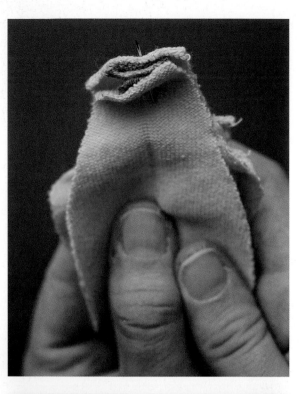

11. Turn your mouse and stuff him. Add tiny black beads for eyes.

pass the excedrin: more challenging projects

Okay. Now I'm not saying these next patterns are going to cause your eyes to bleed or anything, but Dinosaur,* Squirrel, Octopus, and Mermaid *are* challenging. Some of these patterns (Squirrel) are just weird looking (Squirrel). So, you may need extra time to wrap your head around them (Squirrel). But mostly they are just more time-consuming than the other patterns, and you will need to follow my ever-so-clear instructions closely. As long as you know how many legs an octopus is *supposed* to have, you should be fine.

*Not Dino. I lied about that. He's really pretty easy. And fun.

Designed and made by Brenna Maloney

dinosaur

Finished size: about 8½″ long

Who wears toe socks? I mean, really. Unless you are some sort of Pilates master, most of us aren't going to wear them. Most of us like our toes to be together, as a unit. If the truth be told, most of us cannot actually separate our toes. If you move one toe, you move them all. So, naturally, if you own a pair of toe socks—a leftover from your swinging '70s days or something you find in your teenage daughter's sock drawer?—you are going to need something *else* to do with it other than wear it. Which is why I suggest: the Dinosaur.

When I say *dinosaur*, I use that term loosely. He's not really even in the dinosaur ballpark. He's more Bloated-but-Cheerful Sea Monster or Psychedelic Platypus. But, I had to call him something, and Dinosaur is more flattering—so there you are.

I put this project in with the more challenging ones, but don't be fooled; it only *looks* hard. I did that to build your confidence. You will amaze friends, neighbors, and world leaders with this pattern. They will say, "But it looks so complicated!" And you will smile knowingly to yourself because really, it's a snap.

instructions

For information about hand stitching, see page 13.

1. You'll need only 1 toe sock for this pattern.

2. Cut your sock into 3 portions: Cut off the toe section and the cuff. The cuff section should include more than just that nibby bit at the end of the sock; you really want this piece to be about 4" long. Round the middle section slightly while you are cutting to create a slightly narrow nose and a wider back end. This middle section is going to be the body.

3. Turn the cuff end inside out. You're going to freestyle sew yourself a few limbs here—2 legs and 2 arms. Here I've made them about 1" long and rounded the ends, but you could just as easily make them into little triangles, if you like. Cut them out and turn them.

4. Pull out your rotary cutter. In just the top layer of Dino's body, make a slit along the middle of his back the length of the toe section. I've got it tucked in here loosely so you can get the idea of what you'll be doing with it next. (I usually put the end with the largest toe closest to the head.)

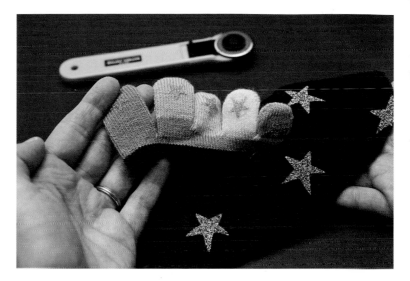

5. To sew, fold the dino's top section in half along that slit, with the toe segment sandwiched between. Machine stitch these layers together from the wrong side.

6. Put the top and bottom body pieces right sides together and sandwich the 4 limbs you made in Step 3 between these, with "feet" pointing inward.

7. Sew all layers together, making sure to leave a small opening to turn Dino. Stuff him and sew up the opening with a slip stitch.

8. Do give him some eyes. I tried to find a small but especially sparkly pair of glass beads.

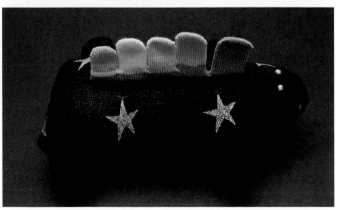

See now? None of that was actually tricky at all, and here you have something that's way more fun than the prospect of keeping your toes separated. Which I still contend is unnatural and, dare I say it? Just plain wrong.

Designed and made by Brenna Maloney

squirrel

Finished size: about 10″ tall

I will confess that Squirrel is one of my favorites. Mostly because I found a few nifty socks that screamed "*Squirrel!*" but also because when my husband looked at it for the first time, he said, "Yeah. Okay. Umm, that one is pretty weird." And it *is* weird. But in a good way. You can have a lot of fun with this pattern, giving him big eyes, strange teeth, and a funky tail. Squirrel can really absorb a lot of your creative impulses.

instructions

For information about hand stitching, see page 13.

1. I found a *ginormously* long sock for this pattern. A standard knee-high will do, of course, and you'll likely only need 1.

2. The heel of this sock will become the face of your squirrel, so cut the foot section off fairly close to the heel, with only 1" or so room to spare. If your sock is crazy long, like mine, you might want to trim the cuff up a bit so his body isn't quite so tall. Up to you on that one.

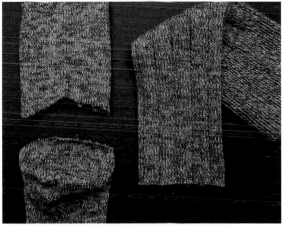

3. You can use the toe to create front paws and ears. Turn the toe section inside out and freehand-sew these items. I like to make the ears a little bulbous on top. The paws are about 1" long.

4. This next step is where the weirdness comes in. Using sections of the sock cuff we cut off already, we're going to create a pair of legs for Squirrel. I've given you a pattern (page 111), but it's really fun to dream up your own. Be sure to leave a small opening at the back of each leg when sewing so you can turn them. Because of the sock I used, these happen to look more like frog legs at this stage. Oh well.

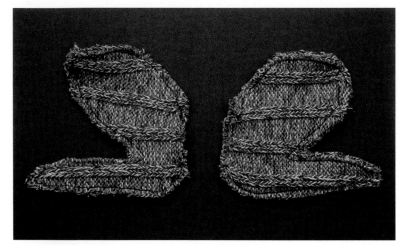

note

I like to give Squirrel great big haunches and long, thin toes. None of mine ever come out looking the same, even when they are for the same squirrel. I think this is fun, but I know it will burn the biscuits off of some of you, so it's perfectly okay to use the pattern and make them consistent.

5. Cut out and turn the paws, ears, and legs.

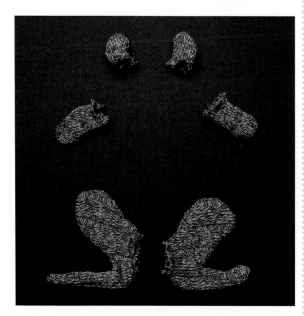

6. We'll work on the head next. Take each ear and fold it over slightly to create a little tuck.

7. Turn Squirrel's body inside out and insert the ears between the layers of his head with the tuck facing forward. Sew his head closed.

8. With his body still inside out, slide a piece of cardboard between his chest and back, and use your trusty rotary cutter to cut two ½" slits in his chest.

9. Now you've got two fine holes where you can put his paws.

With Mr. Squirrel inside out, insert the paws with rounded ends facing inward, and machine sew across them to trap the paws as for Hamster (page 80).

10. Turn Mr. Squirrel right side out and stuff him firmly. You don't want him to be too floppy because then he'll have trouble sitting up.

11. Sew a running stitch around the sock end and pull and knot it to close up his butt.

12. Gently stuff his weird little legs. My squirrel's legs look like green chicken nuggets. I can hardly believe you are following my advice! So far this project looks absurd. But have faith. You don't want to overstuff his legs—he is not Steroid Squirrel— but they should be firm. Stitch them closed with a slip stitch.

13. Sew Squirrel's legs to the sides of his body. His little toesies are going to splay out a bit when you stand him up, but that is fine.

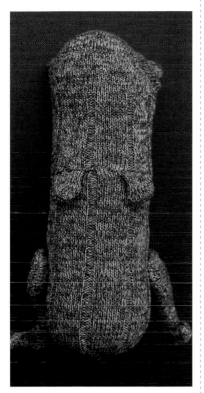

14. He'll need a pair of eyes. I like oval felt eyes for Squirrel, but obviously, you can choose whatever you fancy.

15. On to teeth. Choosing your squirrel's teeth will be a tough decision. I've tried a number of things: Felt, beads, wire. Study his face and audition a few ideas before you sew anything on. Here I used long metal beads with words stamped on them.

16. Your next toughest move is selecting the right tail. The tail can literally be anything, but you want something tall and bushy. I used a coiled-up marabou craft boa.

Coil that sucker a few times, stitch it firmly in place, and Bob's your uncle!

A word about tails

With Squirrel, I tried several materials to create different looks.

Grosgrain gift wrap bow

Coiled feathers

Raffia ribbon, for a really great, unkempt look

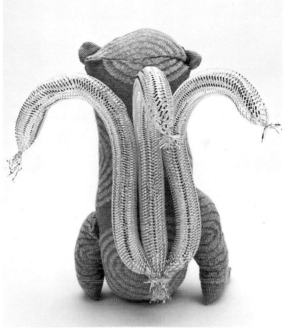

"Stretchy Ribbon," an odd gift-wrapping item I found at The Container Store. This woven, tubular ribbon stretches and springs back into place. I put pipe cleaners inside the ribbon to give it a base and control the way the coils went.

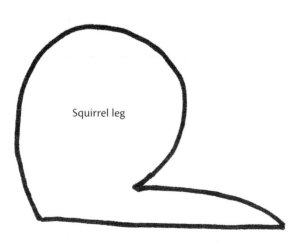

Squirrel leg

Designed and made by Brenna Maloney

octopus

Finished size: about 10″ long (short-armed octopus); 18″ long (long-armed octopus)

Well, didn't this little ole pattern cause dissension in my house! How many arms does an octopus have? Eight, right? How many arms does a squid have? Eight? Or...so? I made the octopus, and someone in the family remarked that her skinny little head made her look more like a squid. "Fine," I said. "We'll call her a squid." But my father said, "You can't call her a squid. She doesn't have enough appendages." Who knew that squids have ten? Well, they have eight "arms" and two other longer thingies called tentacles. Ye gods. So what I've cooked up here is really an eight-armed octopus with a suspicious-looking squid head.

To make matters worse, there are two ways to produce this pattern. One method requires two knee-highs for an octopus with short arms. The other method requires three knee-highs for an octopus with long arms. (And I suppose if you want to be a purist, you can add two more longer thingies on her and just call her a squid and be done with it.)

instructions: short-armed octopus

For information about hand stitching, see page 13.

1. Find yourself two matching knee-highs. I love striped socks for this pattern. Polka dotted ones are great, too.

2. Cut off about 4" of the toe section from your first sock.

3. You'll use the rest of this sock and most of the next sock for arms. They will require some care and patience, I'm afraid. You are going to have to slice, dice, and make julienne fries out of your socks to get enough arms. My particular sock has contrasting bits, so I had to cut off the nibby white bit of the cuff at the end.

4. Cut what is left of your sock cuff into 2 segments of equal length.

5. Now stay with me here. This next bit is rather tricky. Cut each segment into 3 strips of equal width, for a total of 6 strips.

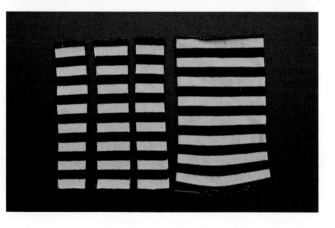

Cut 1 similar-sized segment from your second sock, and cut 2 more strips from the segment to make your total 8. Do you have 8 now? Oh, good. Well, maybe that part wasn't so tricky then. Maybe it's the next bit that's tricky. I can't remember. Let's just keep going and see.

6. Turn each "arm" (strip) inside out (right sides together). On each, stitch along one side, across one end, and up the other side to create a tube. Don't stitch the other end.

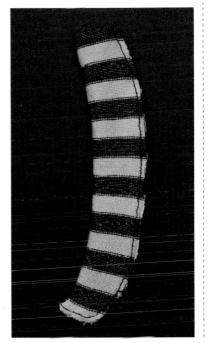

7. Go back to the toe section of your sock and turn it inside out. Sew a large U shape to form Octopus's head. Because my sock has a contrasting toe, I needed to eliminate the white part, so I sewed my U just underneath it.

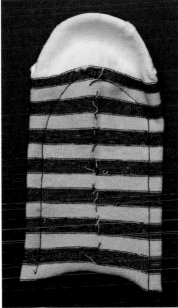

8. Trim the seam allowance to ¼" on the head, then turn it and the arms right side out. Cut a 2" segment from what is remaining of the second sock, and shape it into an oval. This will form her underbelly.

9. Ah, yes! *This* is the tricky part! This is the part that will have you cursing my name. (Get in line on *that* one, sister.) What we want to do is tack the arms in place before we sew on the underbelly. Here's how to do this. Turn her head inside out again. Slowly, slowly tuck each arm inside her head and pin the raw edge of the arm to the edge of her head. Do your best to evenly space them.

10. When you're done pinning, she should look like this.

11. Now slowly, slowly, slowly machine stitch around the edge using a ¼" seam allowance, to lock each arm in place. Stop calling me names. Just work slowly; it's not that bad.

12. The next step will go very smoothly for you. Trim that oval piece I had you cut earlier to fit the hole in her head. Pin it in place and slowly sew around the base, leaving a small opening so you can turn her.

13. Turn her.

14. Get a look at that lovely underbelly!

15. She's ready for a bit of stuffing, which will only go in her head because you've sealed off her arms. This is fine because you want her arms to be flat and floppy. Stitch up the opening with a slip stitch.

16. On to her eyes! I had the best, best luck with these bizarre sequins. My mother found them in a hobby store sale bin. The company that makes them is Horizon Group USA. I have no idea how hard it would be to find them, but I think they make perfect octopus eyes. Large, round sequins will also work; large buttons will work; felt, of course, would work.

17. I know you hate me now, but isn't she marvelous?

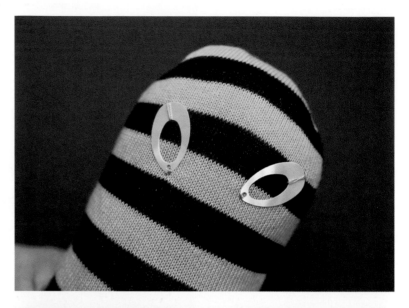

instructions:
long-armed octopus

For information about hand stitching, see page 13.

1. If you are feeling a little crazy and actually want to make an octopus with longer arms, here's the trick. Start with three knee-highs. (The rest is the same as making his short-legged sister.)

2. You might have to study how I cut this out. It's enough to make your eyes bleed, but here we go:

Cut 1 long toe section for the head.

Cut 1 heel for the underbody.

Cut 8 really long strips from the tops of the knee-highs (you will have leftover bits to use for other projects).

3. Now just follow the instructions in Steps 6 through 16 (pages 115–118), as you would to make the short-legged octopus.

Designed and made by Brenna Maloney

mermaid

Finished size: about 9″ tall

What's that? Hear that sound? It's the sound of a siren calling, a sweet mermaid, and she's telling you to go find a couple of pairs of socks.

instructions

For information about hand stitching, see page 13.

1. For Mermaid, you'll need a white sock of any size and a colored sock of any size. You can use whatever color you like: I tend to choose turquoise socks for the mermaid, but that's me.

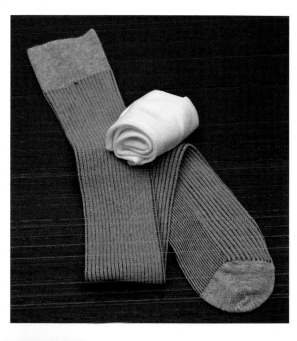

2. Cut a segment about 6" long off the toe and foot part of the colored sock. Cut a 4" segment from the white sock.

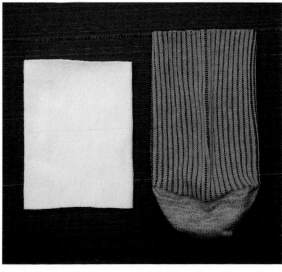

3. Using the patterns on page 125 (or creating your own design), cut out Mermaid's head/torso and tail. Sew the front and back pieces together on each, leaving the *bottom* and *head* of the torso open and the *top* of the tail open. Trim away the excess around the edges.

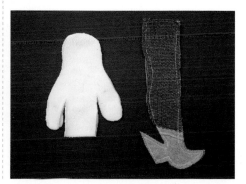

4. Creating Mermaid's hair can be a lot of fun. Look through your yarn collection and see if you have anything wild that might make a good mermaid mane. I found a number of fuzzy craft yarns in blues and turquoises. You can use ribbon, yarn, doll hair, anything.

5. I gathered the selected yarns and cut them into 6" strands, then knotted the strands into clumps. I found that it is slightly easier to sew and keep track of the wild yarn this way. I created 5 clumps of yarn.

6. To get Mermaid's hair in place, push the knotted strands up through her torso until they are peeking out of her open head. Push all 5 clumps in place, spread evenly across the head opening, and pin them in place.

7. Sew across the top of her head to catch all the clumps. Turn her and admire her fine head of hair.

8. Gently stuff her lower and upper halves.

9. Tuck her torso into the tail piece and fold over the top of the tail to create a smooth line across her middle. Use a ladder stitch to connect her upper and lower body.

10. Her eyes can be small beads of any color that suits you. You can try different materials on her chest for modesty. I found some lovely shell sequins at a garage sale that I rather like.

School of Mermaids

To give you an idea of some of the other things you can try, have a look at two more lovely ladies.

I used doll hair on this mermaid. I am sure there is an orderly way to put this type of hair on a doll, and frankly, I would love to know it. I had *sproings* of doll hair all over the place. (I think *sproings* is the technical term for that.) Still, I think it looks rather nice on her, don't you?

For her tail, I wanted to try a stitch on my sewing machine that looked like scales. I was having a devil of a time doing it because my machine was literally eating socks left and right. Then my mother, The Knower of All Things, suggested I back the sock with grocery store freezer paper to give it some stability. It was a clever solution that worked beautifully. Just lay the sock down

on the freezer paper and sew the fancy stitch in a contrasting thread in long rows, then peel away the paper.

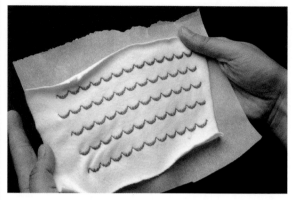

I used two little dried-up starfish from a craft store for her chest.

For another mermaid, I thought I'd brighten the pattern up some by using a pink sock. I left her tail plain, but you could certainly embellish it. I did give her sparkly rhinestone eyes and weird leaf-sequin boobs. I used only one type of yarn for her hair because it was fuzzy and variegated and looked pretty good in a clump.

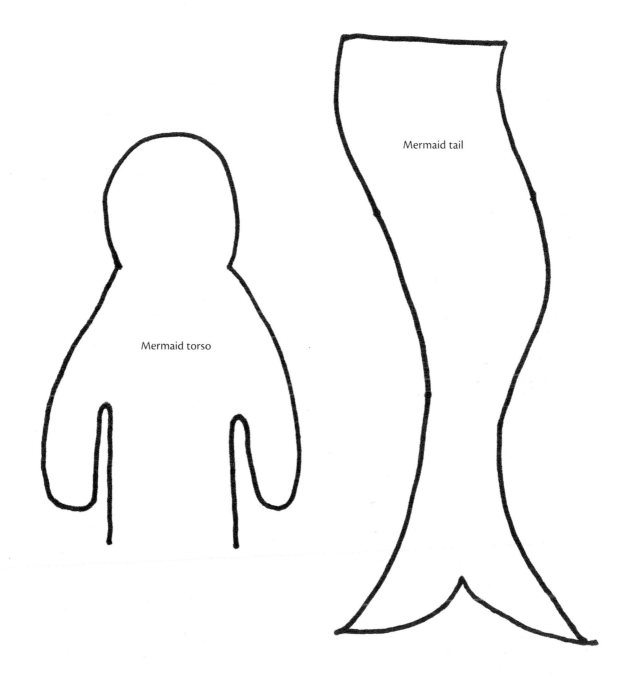

Mermaid torso

Mermaid tail

final thoughts

Uhhhhhh…'bye!

Oh, wait. That's a bit abrupt now, isn't it? Especially after all we've been through together. I've certainly enjoyed spending time with you, and I thank you for using this book. It was very kind of you to buy it or loan it to a friend. Although really, your friend should buy her own. How else am I going to sell enough books to quit my day job?

I hope I've convinced you that socks are *not* for The Wearing on The Feet. Socks have a higher purpose, and now that you have used this book, you should hear the tiny voices of socks calling you, calling you, calling you relentlessly. *"Release me,"* they say! *"Release me from The Drudgery of The Foot. Let me be the Fish, the Hamster, the Rabbit, the Lion!"*

So, go forth and do as instructed, my friend. Be brave! And if— when you're in your lair, sewing away—a brilliant idea strikes you for a new sock pattern, let me know. Send me the pattern, and I'll give it a try. You'd be amazed at how much fun it is to dream these things up. And it's the least I can do after torturing you with mine! Here's how to reach me: www.socksappeal.org

Until next time,

Brenna

about the author

By day, Brenna is an award-winning journalist. A long time editor for *The Washington Post*, she is currently editor of *National Geographic Explorer* magazine. By night, Brenna stays up late making odd things from socks and eating entirely too many Junior Mints. She lives in Washington, D.C. with her husband and two young sons. She was last seen stalking socks at a local Target store. Here's how to reach her: www.socksappeal.org

---

For a list of other fine books from C&T Publishing, ask for a free catalog:

C&T PUBLISHING, INC.

P.O. Box 1456
Lafayette, CA 94549
800-284-1114

Email: ctinfo@ctpub.com
Website: www.ctpub.com

C&T Publishing's professional photography services are now available to the public. Visit us at www.ctmediaservices.com.

Tips and Techniques can be found at www.ctpub.com > Consumer Resources > Quiltmaking Basics: Tips & Techniques for Quiltmaking & More

For sewing supplies:

COTTON PATCH

1025 Brown Ave.
Lafayette, CA 94549
Store: 925-284-1177
Mail order: 925-283-7883

Email: CottonPa@aol.com
Website: www.quiltusa.com

stashBOOKS

fabric arts for a handmade lifestyle

If you're craving beautiful authenticity in a time of mass-production...StashBooks is for you. StashBooks is a new line of how-to books celebrating fabric arts for a handmade lifestyle. Backed by C&T Publishing's solid reputation for quality, StashBooks will inspire you with contemporary designs, clear and simple instructions, and engaging photography.

www.stashbooks.com